Birds and Bruises

Birds and Bruises

Poems by

Vanessa Napolitano

Cover design by Shay Culligan
Cover photo by Jim Gatehouse-Cross
Author photo by Lilith Napolitano

ISBN: 978-1-63980-614-0

Kelsay Books
502 South 1040 East, A-119
American Fork, Utah 84003
Kelsaybooks.com

For Stephen, Lilith, and Katherine

Acknowledgments

Thank you to the following publications, in which versions of these poems previously appeared:

Iaminprint competition: "Summer, Los Angeles"
Leeds Poetry Festival anthology: "Ash Wednesday, Los Angeles 2017"
Poetry Wales: "The List"

With thanks to Kayla Cagan and Leila Howland whose writing group support has kept me going for over 14 years.

Contents

Follow your

If I have to have a heart,
can it be a cauliflower heart
bedded in pale green leaves,
bloodless and broad,
     a substitute
for meat?

     can it be
an artichoke—a thing best served
before it blooms,

or a heart of palm, a clean stem
harvested from a tree,
presented like a reprimand.

Can I be commanded by the sun,
by thirst, turn what feeds us
green?

This clumsy mammal clockwork.
How we need it to stay alive.
How it raps out our decisions-

decide, decide, decide.

Whipped

I thought about making a trifle,
the red glossy jelly trembling
on a sponge mattress slick in sherry,
whipping cream on setting two until it thickened,
custard from the Bird's tin made and cooled. No fruit in the trifle,
no matter what the guests said.

You can argue whether hundreds & thousands
ought to be sprinkles or jimmies as I shake them on top
like fairy dust.

My mother might still have the glass bowl
flower-etched that sat on the sideboard,
though the serving spoon recedes. I imagine a soup ladle,
a silver boat. A stack of smaller bowls, receiving.

All I really want is the ladyfingers from the packet,
unsoaked, uncrumbled. To watch the cream thicken.
Somebody else's labour.

Nothing in between.

Bruise

Sky is like a bruise I once got rollerskating,
I went down hard and the blood
softly rainbowed under my skin.

Sky does it faster, sharp quick blood,
then all pastel softness,
before the dull lightness
makes you doubt it was ever there.

Sky we pull forward, tug back,
to set the daylight hours to our liking.
Spring, and Fall, and restive children
waking up to a clock their body conjures.

Sky, when it is cold there is no paucity of stars,
when it is hot you seem to never succumb.
I have never learned how to balance, and glide.

This morning

Next door's cat eyes the fat magpies.
I anticipate laundry from a nest of blankets
whilst my daughter watches pirates and children dressed as pirates.

Next door's cat relaxes in a fat slat of sunlight.
No feathers flutter down. No sheets whip in the wind. No unrest.
My daughter is a ballerina in purple.

I fold the blanket. I stretch like the cat, I think about the plants I
don't tend. The pirates walk a plank to a slime pool resplendent in
green.

I fold my skin and slip outside and fly around with the magpies.
Count us through the window. I'm sunlight and sticks. Trees and
billow.
The cycle stops. Hang it out to dry.

Witch Stone

For years I cried over a pebble
blue threaded with the purple drops where my tears stained,

these were witch tears.
The pebble grew without consent into a boulder.

This boulder cast shade. I caught my breath.
It rolled downhill and ruined the homes of my enemies.

I followed. A stone grown in sorrow.
It grew a fissure that became a cave.

I lived inside counting magpies until I saw
two for joy. No more, no less.

Walking out, the pebble became itself, hopping
on to the palm of my hand.

It is in my pocket now. Smooth. Small.
Sharp.

Skeleton Key

They worked all night to make a skeleton key
to unlock the invisible door
where your memories live,
but the ivy was so tangled
and the carpets were too thick
and now we're both trying to remember who you were.

You called the speaking clock to remind you of the time,
to make a frame of seconds to build yourself around
but you dropped the hours and minutes
when the receiver clicked down,
and now the shop is shut.

We took you in, we took you home,
the walls, the floors, all unknown
we showed you your objects, one by one,
ring, rug, book, chair,
oh bird outside, that was once there,

sing her back to herself,
but the magpies have also flown.
These children who keep visiting
carrying stacks of words
have unfamiliar faces
and burdens that are not theirs.

They worked all night to make a skeleton key,
though they found the lock vanished.

Now we can only cloak you in kindness,
oh bird outside
that was once there.

The Leader

A man as tender as the underside of a scab
lost in a forest with his pen knife. Cutting himself free.
Screaming respect me respect me respectme.
The dense tall proud trees,
the new foliage, the twisted vines. Hateful to him, all of it.
He wishes for flat blank land. He wishes for land before trees,
Before canopies of leaves. He's choking at his podium. Bring him
    water. Where was I?

A man lost in a forest with his pen knife, picking at a scab.
He's afraid. He found a tribe of terrified people and threw a rock,
and now the habit has stuck, strike loose the bark.
Harpoon the birds. Grand gestures. Big fires. He had an argument
    with a magpie,
straightened his tie. Wouldn't shake hands. Just remember—

He can't do it, can't name the trees that make our fabric,
Custard Apple, Netleaf Hackberry, Noble Fir,
Sierra Live Oak, Desert Palm. I love you all.
He's toxic and naked with fear and flame and yelling.
He's a blunt axe that brings no relief.
Pass him his water. Pass him on by.

Tree Bones

What's the difference? Forest, woods,
a darkening of trees amassed,
defined only by extent. The short sharp trail
through to the canal path is a woods. The National Park we drove
    through,
winding in dusk, forest. But now I think it's more,
a kind of hinge of malevolence and magic depending on the
    density
and lean of the trees. A woods is for picnics and earnest fairy tales.
A forest is for axes, eyes, plots. A forest is not the same thing
at night. You're not right to be scared.
You're right to be scared.
Old trees, tall trees, wiry skeleton trees, industrial trees.
Their strength is in numbers;
they prevent the sky.

Pattern-Seeker

I will carry any charms, I will drink any potion,
I will light any candles. Please. I am the pattern-seeker,
the rule-follower, the box-ticker. My vanity in conformity is
    legendary.
I have kept the lock of hair, the root of marigold, the shell from the
    beach.
I have said the incantation every night before I sleep.
I have counted in sevens. I have turned three times to the right.
And still my organs vibrate, and still my bones buzz, and still
    nothing is.
Still.
I will visualise. I will list. I will circle it in stones.
I will write it down and pin it to a board.
I will imagine my good golden self, serene. Look how she floats,
look how she folds into a yoga pose, look how she folds the
    laundry.
I will walk once around the block. Bathe in the tree shadow.
Journal and gratitude it. Smile and platitude it.
And still the magpies circle. And still my skin prickles. And still
    nothing is.

Paper Birds

I wasn't there when you made them
I don't know the species
or the details of their flight.

Just them flat against the table.
Paint and pen,
scissor and feather.

Just you painting on the glass,
imagining the wings
that fly in currents of laughter.

I thought about how daughters
once fit beneath our ribs
like gentle origami

I thought about how the smallest cuts
are made by paper
when we are busy shaping.

I hope one day you're sorting art
as mothers often do and
that bird flies from the pile

and gives today back to you.

If your words were hummingbirds

If your words were wire
I would worry the metal strands
into a statement necklace,
I would wear your sentences
around the office
as an explanation.

If your words were wool
I would knit them into a huge blanket
as cosy as cocoa in winter
and I would hide beneath it,
safe,
and just a little too warm.

If you words were flour
I would bake them and eat them,
they would power me through the day
and my internal systems
would recognize sustenance from waste.

If your words were money
we'd both know what they were worth.

If your words were hummingbirds
I would open my windows,
I would send them out to the streets of Los Angeles
where people would find them beautiful
and unnervingly fast
like a heartbeat outside a body
and I'd tell them
now you know!

If your words were fact
we'd call this science,
and it would make sense
that the world
          essentially shifts
when you talk.

Headspace

Birds origami the sky and slice open the morning,
gushing extravagant light into coffee grounds,
eggs turning from translucence to breakfast,
text turning from plain words to sour news.

A rocket turns on a pedestal, a pivot
sending back data, this light old, star-dead,
now showing in the morning newsreel.
Toast turns to astronauts' ice-cream in our mouths.

Which boundary to live inside, these walls
with their sense, gentle geometry of home,
or this whole world, connection and trauma,
fizzing from its inputs? Brittle,

we the protected filter, and hold how much to absorb,
pulling the curtains on, turning the broadcast off.
Still, the rocket turns, transmits;
still the birds shriek through these thin windows.

Dandelion Clocks

Extravagant weeds chokehold my garden,
my mascara is smeared. Edges are not precise.
In my capable body that carries itself through the days
I once knit your bones and nourished you,
and now you stand separate, holding a spade and pulling up
the yellow dandelions.

Extravagant yellow dandelions spread like fire.
My naked face turns up to sunshine. Hours are not precise.
In your capable body that carries you through the days
I see the pattern of your bones, how though
separate from me you are connected forever,
pulling apart the dandelion clocks.

Extravagant dandelion clocks spread their spores.
We lock eyes as they dance. Our love is precise.
Our bodies are capable still of this connection,
integral to one another in patterns of growth,
filling the space together, this garden, our hearts,
dancing together in yellow dandelions.

Glossolalia

How to say that the birds speak in tongues?
and the sky's haphazard symbols are codes.
pecking for meaning in the runes I have flung.

in such chaos as the dandelion seeds, a cure for all wrongs—
in acorns and chestnuts no ill meaning bodes.
How to say that the birds speak in tongues-

they call for understanding, but nobody comes.
all the dappled roof of trees spell out their odes
pecking for meaning in the runes I have flung

and in flinging for fate, what have I done?
tipped the first fury out on their road.
How to say that the birds speak in tongues

and poke at what wants them, and what doesn't they shun
and some seeds are blooming, and some were not sewn
How to say birds speak in tongues,
pecking for meaning in the runes I have flung.

Salton Sea

Before,
Sinatra sang across the waters. Yachts moored and twinkled.
Binoculars and fishing were rife.

Then, scientists said, agricultural runoff. Imbalance. Catastrophic
    decline.
The community blinked.

Because nobody listened, you continued to shrink,
your evaporated shoreline stinking clouds of
toxic air.
Nobody seemed to care. Beers around the edge? Yes, friend.
All the fish died in the basin and the birds, once such a draw,
were no more.

There was a project and a project to manage the project.
A documentary. A counterintuitive tourist movement. A decorative
    mug.
An Act and an effort.
Little and late. Little and late.
Here you remain, home only to the desert pupfish.
Saline. Stench. No birdsong, no Sinatra.

Myself

How like myself
to explain too much,
to talk too loud at parties
jamming my words, a foot in the door of your pause.

Look, I've brought you a present;
a cat that brought you a bird could not be more eager
for your approval.

Even though you've already made it clear
that where I camp, you camp
here I am always with the questions,
needing someone to keep the matches dry.

How like myself
I am,
how happy I am
that you don't mind at all.

Not the flowers, nor birds either

I don't know the names. I looked them up.
Not bluebells, not daffodils, not the ones I had already met,
Silene-Chalcedonica,Gentiana Verna, the ones I haven't learned
    yet, or couldn't
possibly identify in a field, on a sight-seeing trip—if you pushed
    me and said;
What about this? And that? Those small, delicate yellow ones?

Oh, you mean a dandelion?
No? I don't know the names of them, I looked them up,
the common cotton-grass, the Bilberry, vulgar names and local.
They'll change no doubt, give them just a season, if it ever stops
    snowing,
Though I don't know that either, the where and when they flourish,

the quality of soil, what nourishes them, in what weather
they would freeze and spoil. Papaver Rhoeas, Silene Nutans.
Wouldn't it be nicer, on our woodland walks if I knew?
But I'm sorry darling,
I don't know the names of them. I looked them up

because of the garden, what could we grow—nothing wild,
nothing delicate, nothing careful, nothing that needs me
to rake up the stones (even the stones can be called something
particular) or pull up the weeds or water them much;

I don't know the name of it, but I can look it up.

What I did within the days till they brightened

Rinsed them in light rain,
clipped off the dead wood.
Scraped off the frost,
watched dirty foam
rush downriver.
Saw the evenings elongate,
sliding in wedges of light
as sharp as lemon slices.
Shook myself off in a field
like a golden lab. Ran away.
Came home. Splintered a block of chocolate
into fragments and melted them into cake.
Watched for signs of blossom.
Slept and dreamt of seeds sprouting.
Felt the Spring static in the bones of everything.
Hummed. Knew myself to be green.

Spring, lovestruck

Blossom starts to bud, that's how I know
that you are almost born again, back in time.
You laid claim to the whole season, milk-fresh, thirsty and new.

On our first walk outside together I am an ache,
pale-faced, and you clutch nothing in your tiny fingers, against
    your cheek,
as if still suspended inside me.
Jacaranda and palm trees and so much love I feel I will fall to
    pieces and float.
A suspended heart. Only the weight of you on my chest later held
    me down.

How was it I had become so heavy and you came and cancelled
    gravity?

Blossom starts to bud, that's how I remember.
Ibuprofen every six hours,
sleepless every two,
you and I survey the city skyline,
float underneath the trees, and this belongs only to us.

Here comes the Spring.
Cherry blossoms on the street corner.
A blue sky.
Everything in the world means more because you exist.

Oh /what an /April it is

I
feed you
just banana bread

Imagine
the danishes
the cafe makes.

Easter
hops along,
eggs amongst daffodils

out
you come
with your basket

excited,
blue foil
pink foil, chocolate.

We
never were
very religious people.

Mother
I'm glad
I know prayer

though.
Time was
girls in yellow

Danced
Spring dances
on the lawn;

time
we know
is very fickle.

Cambridge, 2004

River drinking itself in night and orange light,
Students whooping on grass somewhere,

Walk me home from the basement of our past
Up to a certain bridge, from which the tentacles of

Future selves brush against the water.
Problems like boats sailing out,

Some of them never meant to float. There was a time
When my hair was shorter than yours

And your golden hoop earrings were stolen,
When I didn't think of how many units I had drunk

Or where the wine was from. This was our lives about to start,
As if already a treadmill wasn't moving

Beneath us more quickly than our hearts beat
(we knew everything, didn't we?)

(we know everything now?)
So I go back and it's delicious, everything-

Our righteous walk home, our inebriation
Our idea of control even in the dark, even over rushing water.

Ash Wednesday, April 2017, Los Angeles

Hot wind bending palm trees into bows,
women streaming from the hospital chapel with ash on their brows,
forgiven.

Feeling the slightness of fever in the stickiness of your underarms,
the way you push your spoon away.

I ate nothing but pancakes just before Lent,
now the pressure is rising all around,
how different. That day I was thinking mainly about kinds of syrup
    and kinds of giving up.
Listen,

just when you think it can't rain, distantly the clouds gather around
    a mountain
and a stranger says *someone is really getting it now.*

*

You're not this hot loaf of bread I bought. It's still hot through the
    paper,
touch it.
You're not these yellow roses. I have things. I want things. Tiny
    macaroons
with rose paste and crispy shells. Tall cold glasses of prosecco.
Someone to push me just one inch more.
You're not my high high expectations. Not my problems.
I have a loaf. I have a knife.
I have an idea.

*

These wingless birds singing on the lean branches outside
only remember you as a child,
only sing of the ineffable sadness
of your eventual flight.

They would still like to be picking the grit from your feathers;
they would like a way inside.

The list

They'll come like enchanted godmothers
wise and calm
now the blood rush of their own newborns has settled,
carrying advice and veiled favour.

Amongst their offerings is the list
of all that you should do now.

Symphonies of sleep,
pearls of milk,
nets of nurture, of knowing,
spells for every second of growing.

Muslin for miles,
forests of fatigue,
lights and temperatures
calibrated for your evaluation.

Tales meant to be an education.
A sisterhood of witches, well-meaning;
A noisy village that can't stop interfering.
You, my darling, riding waves of advice—

please
just do
what your gut says is right.

Landlocked

Your birthday is landlocked and sun-drenched.
Eight years ago I was in Portland, almost thirty,

I was eight years younger, thin, almost thirty.
Blonde. Would you have known your mother then?

My mother was diagnosed with cancer then,
I spoke to her on the steps of Portland Museum of Art

I also only imagine steps at Portland Museum of Art
Memory is fickle, like the party balloons-

we have festooned the room in balloons
I'm trying to thread today with light

even as some days it's hard to find light
I'm glad of cake, I'm glad of levity

Of people phoning to add levity
Your birthday is landlocked and sun-drenched.

Summer, Los Angeles

Deciding on brunch, powdered sugar on pancakes,
not minding forty minute queues for mimosas,
not thinking about a two mile walk there, a two mile walk back.
Our limbs pinked by the sun, never sunscreen in my extra bag,
never an extra bag,
less time given to contingencies.

If we were tired we napped on the sofa
with our jaws slack and the dog curled
in the apostrophe of our knees,

at the edges of my days happy hours,
late night trips to the pharmacy or supermarket,
street lights and bedtimes unhooked from one another.
Trees a corset on the spine of the street and the city back then
was mine, safe, unsafe, who cared

about property prices and extra rooms
and where the good schools were.

There was time for wanting,
that became a sort of cage,

until the Summer I saw your beginning,
and everything changed.

Florida

It's not the turquoise of the pool or the abundance of green I think of. Partly it's the train from the terminal with its robot doors and the tourists pulling fat suitcases through. Initially it's the first-night hotel we stay in, so cold with room-service poké bowls and white sheets and busy carpets.

Mainly it's the ink-black nights blotting out the ocean sunset. The moon in the ocean. The ocean shushing in the dark. We walk to the edge of the jetty. We are so far from home for me, so close to childhood for you. I fear mosquitoes. You are immune.

We kiss by water, tradition founded early, now enjoyed in abundance.

Leaning out of the rental car window I see the clouds, tall, magnificent. Florida skies! I say. You smile. Iced pumpkin spice lattes. Peanut m & ms between us. A roll of quarters for the tolls.

Hiking in marshes in heat
I can. Barely think straight in.

This isn't our honeymoon. It's not uncharted territory. I want to go to the big Target and see alligators. It's Florida. Mainly, it's the ink-black nights.

Mainly it's your silhouette against water that I think of.

About the Author

Vanessa Napolitano is a dual British-American citizen and Pushcart nominated poet whose writing is informed by strong associations of place and time. She has a Masters in Poetry from MMU and a love of folklore. Her recent publications can be found in *Poetry Wales, Trees, Seas & Attitudes* anthology, *Mom Egg Review's Summer Folio,* and *Free Verse Revolution* journal. Her poetry was longlisted for the Leeds Festival Poetry prize in 2023, as well as placing third in the 2023 *I am in print* poetry competition.

www.ingramcontent.com/pod-product-compliance
Lightning Source LLC
Chambersburg PA
CBHW051434090426
42737CB00014B/2978